This book belongs to

_____

_____

Includes 2 each of 25 Goddess and Mythology coloring images by Selina Fenech.

As an artist, color is a thing of magic in my life. Color creates shapes, forms, and feelings in the artworks I paint. Laying color onto a blank page is when I feel closest to true magic, when I feel happiest and most relaxed, and it's through what I create that I share my love of magic with the world. Through my coloring books I want to share that same magic with you.

The artworks in my books are based on my completed paintings, which I have painted over the last ten years as a professional artist. I have created the coloring designs to be a mix of intricate and detailed while still fun and accessible. There is something for lovers of meditative detail while simple enough to not be overwhelming for younger colorists.

When designing my books I decided to print them with two copies of each design, because as an artist I know there are always so many possibilities! I also wanted to give everybody the chance of a do-over with every design in case of an oops (as an artist I know that happens too!). Try a different medium, or a different colour scheme. Or share the magic with a friend, child, parent, or sibling. Because sharing your creativity and joy of color is the best magic of all.

See the colors the artist chose for her paintings at www.selinafenech.com

Goddess and Mythology Coloring Book
by Selina Fenech
First Published July 2016
Published by Fairies and Fantasy PTY LTD
ISBN: 978-0-9945852-2-6

Using This Book

 Turn off and move away from distractions. Relax into the peaceful process of coloring and enjoy the magic of these fantasy images.

 Experiment! There is no right or wrong way to color, and with two of each image, there's no pressure.

 This book works best with color pencils or markers. Wet mediums should be used sparingly. Slip a piece of card behind the image you're working on in case the markers bleed through.

 Don't be scared to dismantle this book. Cut finished pages out to frame, or split the book in half where the second set of images start so you and a loved one can color together.

 Never run out of fantasy coloring pages by signing up to Selina's newsletter. Get free downloadable pages and updates on new books at - selinafenech.com/free-coloring-sampler/

Share Your Work

  Share on Instagram with **#colorselina** to be included in Selina's coloring gallery, and visit the gallery for inspiration.

selinafenech.com/coloringgallery

"Valkyrie"

From Norse mythology, Valkyrie are women who watch over battles and choose who lives or dies. They then take their chosen dead warriors to the halls of Valhalla.

"Blodeuwedd"

In Welsh mythology, Blodeuwedd was made from flowers by two magicians to become the wife of Lleu Llaw Gyffes. In one story she is transformed into an owl.

"Diana"

The Roman goddess of the hunt, moon, and nature, similar to
the Greek goddess, Artemis.

"The Lady of the Lake"

The ruler of Avalon from Arthurian mythology. She is known
for giving King Arthur his sword, and being one of the three
queens to take his body to Avalon when he dies. Is known by
many names including Nimue, Viviane, and Nyneve.

"Arianrhod"

Welsh Goddess Arianrhod is sometimes said to have a palace in the sky. She is shown surrounded by her symbolic silver rings, the moon has the Triskele symbol on it, and the stars on her forehead are the constellation Corona Borealis, known as Caer Arianrhod in Welsh.

"Aphrodite"

Greek goddess of love and sensuality, Aphrodite is often shown with oceanic symbols, and some tales say she was born from sea foam. She was a great beauty and the centre of many scandals.

"Antheia"

One of the Graces of Greek mythology, Antheia is the goddess
of flowers and wreaths and is normally shown in golden tones.

"Athena"

Shrewd, just, and heroic, Athena is a major Greek goddess
of many traits including wisdom, courage, justice, strength,
strategy, and creativity.

"Cerridwen"

From Welsh mythology, Cerridwen mothered a son with disfigured looks, who she hoped to benefit by brewing a potion to give him great intelligence and inspiration. When the first three potent drops of this potion were stolen, she chased the thief by changing into different animal forms, shown in this artwork. The Awen symbol of the three magic drops is seen in the cauldron's surface.

"Coventina"

A Roman-British goddess of wells and springs, she holds a
magical chalice of healing.

"Fidelma"

From Irish mythology, Fidelma is a seer and bard who was called upon by Goddess-Queen Medb for guidance. She is described in legends as a golden-haired beauty with great intelligence and, like most oracles, not always appreciated honesty.

"Gaia"

A primal goddess of the earth, originating from Greek mythology
and since then being adopted and re-imagined into many faiths
and versions, including the neo-pagan where she is the spiritual
embodiment of the earth itself.

"His Goddess, Her God"

From Wiccan lore, this portrait of the horned god and goddess showing their closeness, equality, and intimacy of relationship can be displayed either way up, with either the god or goddess as the dominant figure.

"Ishtar"

Ishtar is the Babylonian goddess of love, war, dance and sex. She is often depicted with lions and tales tell of her riding into battle on the back of a lion. Ishtar is associated with the moon and Sumerian goddess Inanna.

"Isis"

Egyptian goddess of health, marriage, and wisdom, Isis is told
to have resurrected her husband Osiris by travelling into the
underworld to retrieve his body parts.

"Nüwa"

Also known as Nügua, she is the dragon or snake goddess in ancient
Chinese mythology who created mankind.

"*Selene*"

Selene is the Greek goddess of the moon and many other mythologies have a female embodiment of the moon, including Roman Luma.

"Parvati and Shiva"

The Hindu goddess of fertility, love and devotion as well as of divine strength and power. She is the mother goddess in Hinduism and wife to Shiva, with whom she has a deep romantic bond.

"Tempestas"

The ancient Roman goddess of storms.

"Echo"

A nymph from Greek mythology, Echo was cursed to only be able to speak the last words spoken to her. When she fell in love with Narcissus, the curse humilated her. Lovelorn, Echo wasted away in a cave until nothing was left of her but her voice. She is shown here with Narcissus flowers.

"Guanyin"

The East Asian goddess of compassion and mercy.

"The Triple Goddess"

In many mythologies a single goddess can be shown as having three aspects or forms,
or three goddesses can be so closely tied they are considered one being. This is often
shown in the form of the Maiden, Mother, and Crone.
The Morrigan of Irish mythology is one such goddess, shown here with crow feathers
and the waning, full, and waxing moon symbols.

"Oshun"

Oshun is a deity of rivers and fresh water. She represents all things beautiful and sensual, including love, pleasure, sexuality, fertility, and luxury. From the African Yoruba religion.

"Rhiannon"

A Welsh goddess-queen, Rhiannon is often associated with Epona due to their connection with horses. She is shown here riding a mare with a foal by their side to symbolise her themes of motherhood, and nightingales and bells at the horses ankles for her connection to music. On the hill in the background, the famous Uffington White Horse is visible.

A symbolic image showing the horned god and goddess of Wiccan faith backed by the famous pentagram. The image has a yin-yang style design, contrasting male and female, sun and moon, spring and autumn, and is designed to be shown either way up so either the god or goddess can be dominant, or turned to the side for equality.

Second Set of Pages Begins Here

When designing my books I decided to print them with two copies of each design, because as an artist I know there are always so many possibilities! I also wanted to give everybody the chance of a do-over with every design in case of an oops (as an artist I know that happens too!). Try a different medium, or a different colour scheme. Create without fear! Or share the magic with a loved one. Because sharing your creativity and joy of color is the best magic of all. ~ *Selina*

"Valkyrie"

From Norse mythology, Valkyrie are women who watch over battles and choose who lives or dies. They then take their chosen dead warriors to the halls of Valhalla.

"Blodeuwedd"

In Welsh mythology, Blodeuwedd was made from flowers by two magicians to become the wife of Lleu Llaw Gyffes. In one story she is transformed into an owl.

"Diana"

The Roman goddess of the hunt, moon, and nature, similar to
the Greek goddess, Artemis.

"The Lady of the Lake"

The ruler of Avalon from Arthurian mythology. She is known for giving King Arthur his sword, and being one of the three queens to take his body to Avalon when he dies. Is known by many names including Nimue, Viviane, and Nyneve.

"Arianrhod"

Welsh Goddess Arianrhod is sometimes said to have a palace in the sky. She is shown surrounded by her symbolic silver rings, the moon has the Triskele symbol on it, and the stars on her forehead are the constellation Corona Borealis, known as Caer Arianrhod in Welsh.

"Aphrodite"

Greek goddess of love and sensuality, Aphrodite is often shown with oceanic symbols, and some tales say she was born from sea foam. She was a great beauty and the centre of many scandals.

"Antheia"

One of the Graces of Greek mythology, Antheia is the goddess
of flowers and wreaths and is normally shown in golden tones.

"Athena"

Shrewd, just, and heroic, Athena is a major Greek goddess
of many traits including wisdom, courage, justice, strength,
strategy, and creativity.

"Cerridwen"

From Welsh mythology, Cerridwen mothered a son with disfigured looks, who she hoped to benefit by brewing a potion to give him great intelligence and inspiration. When the first three potent drops of this potion were stolen, she chased the thief by changing into different animal forms, shown in this artwork. The Awen symbol of the three magic drops is seen in the cauldron's surface.

"Coventina"

A Roman-British goddess of wells and springs, she holds a
magical chalice of healing.

"Fidelma"

From Irish mythology, Fidelma is a seer and bard who was called upon by Goddess-Queen Medb for guidance. She is described in legends as a golden-haired beauty with great intelligence and, like most oracles, not always appreciated honesty.

"Gaia"

A primal goddess of the earth, originating from Greek mythology and since then being adopted and re-imagined into many faiths and versions, including the neo-pagan where she is the spiritual embodiment of the earth itself.

"His Goddess, Her God"

From Wiccan lore, this portrait of the horned god and goddess showing their closeness, equality, and intimacy of relationship can be displayed either way up, with either the god or goddess as the dominant figure.

"Ishtar"

Ishtar is the Babylonian goddess of love, war, dance and sex. She is often depicted with lions and tales tell of her riding into battle on the back of a lion. Ishtar is associated with the moon and Sumerian goddess Inanna.

"Isis"

Egyptian goddess of health, marriage, and wisdom, Isis is told to have resurrected her husband Osiris by travelling into the underworld to retrieve his body parts.

"Nüwa"

Also known as Nügua, she is the dragon or snake goddess in ancient Chinese mythology who created mankind.

"Selene"

Selene is the Greek goddess of the moon and many other mythologies have a female embodiment of the moon, including Roman Luma.

"Parvati and Shiva"

The Hindu goddess of fertility, love and devotion as well as of divine strength and power. She is the mother goddess in Hinduism and wife to Shiva, with whom she has a deep romantic bond.

"Tempestas"

The ancient Roman goddess of storms.

"Echo"

A nymph from Greek mythology, Echo was cursed to only be able to speak the last words spoken to her. When she fell in love with Narcissus, the curse humilated her. Lovelorn, Echo wasted away in a cave until nothing was left of her but her voice. She is shown here with Narcissus flowers.

"Guanyin"

The East Asian goddess of compassion and mercy.

"The Triple Goddess"

In many mythologies a single goddess can be shown as having three aspects or forms,
or three goddesses can be so closely tied they are considered one being. This is often
shown in the form of the Maiden, Mother, and Crone.
The Morrigan of Irish mythology is one such goddess, shown here with crow feathers
and the waning, full, and waxing moon symbols.

"Oshun"

Oshun is a deity of rivers and fresh water. She represents all things beautiful and sensual, including love, pleasure, sexuality, fertility, and luxury. From the African Yoruba religion.

"Rhiannon"

A Welsh goddess-queen, Rhiannon is often associated with Epona due to their connection with horses. She is shown here riding a mare with a foal by their side to symbolise her themes of motherhood, and nightingales and bells at the horses ankles for her connection to music. On the hill in the background, the famous Uffington White Horse is visible.

"Wicca"

A symbolic image showing the horned god and goddess of Wiccan faith backed by the famous pentagram. The image has a yin-yang style design, contrasting male and female, sun and moon, spring and autumn, and is designed to be shown either way up so either the god or goddess can be dominant, or turned to the side for equality.

About the Artist

As a lover of all things fantasy, Selina has made a living as an artist since she was 23 years old selling her magical creations. Her works range from oil paintings to oracle decks, dolls to digital scrapbooking, plus Young Adult novels, jewelry, and coloring books.

Born in 1981 to Australian and Maltese parents, Selina lives in Australia with her husband, daughter, and growing urban farm menagerie.

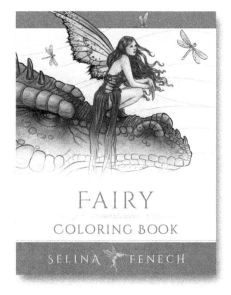

FAIRY
COLORING BOOK
SELINA FENECH

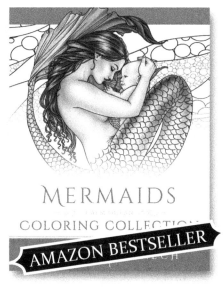

MERMAIDS
COLORING COLLECTION
AMAZON BESTSELLER

GOTHIC
DARK FANTASY
COLORING BOOK
AMAZON BESTSELLER

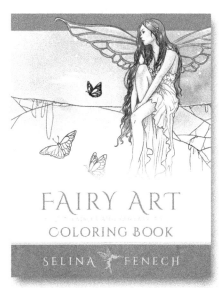

FAIRY ART
COLORING BOOK
SELINA FENECH

MAGICAL
MINIS
POCKET SIZED FAIRY FANTASY ART
COLORING BOOK
SELINA FENECH

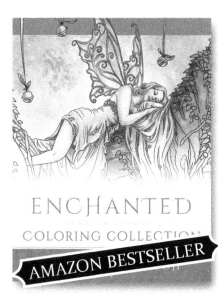

ENCHANTED
COLORING COLLECTION
AMAZON BESTSELLER

See all books online at viewauthor.at/sfcolor

Share Your Work

Selina loves to see your finished designs and the colors you chose!
Share online with **#colorselina**

www.facebook.com/selinafenechart
www.selinafenech.com

CPSIA information can be obtained
at www.ICGtesting.com
Printed in the USA
LVHW100704070321
680755LV00004B/77